ADRIANA LUNA CARLOS
Editor-In-Chief, Designer
and Co-Founder

HANNA OLIVAS
Managing Editor
& Co-Founder

NICOLE CURTIS
Director of the SRS
Magazine Division

FENIX INNOVATION
MAGAZINE

**ADVERTISING
OPPORTUNITIES**
Info@SheRisesStudios.com

FENIX INNOVATION *AUGUST 2024*

**SHE RISES
STUDIOS**

CONTACT US
SheRisesStudios@gmail.com
www.SheRisesStudios.com

www.SheRisesStudios.com

LETTER FROM THE EDITORS

Dear Readers,

Welcome to the August 2024 edition of FENIX Innovation Magazine! This month, we are thrilled to present a dynamic blend of creativity, technology, and business, showcasing the visionaries who are redefining digital media and pioneering new frontiers in the arts. We are excited to unveil this special edition with Ruth Fae gracing our cover—a beacon of intuitive storytelling and transformative publishing.

Ruth Fae, the founder of Fae Blood Publications, epitomizes the innovative spirit we celebrate at FENIX. Her journey from copywriting to becoming a renowned Intuitive Writing Coach is a testament to the power of aligning passion with purpose. Ruth's dedication to helping silenced voices find their authentic expression through storytelling is both inspiring and impactful, and we are honored to share her story with you
.

In this issue, we dive deep into the realms of digital media, exploring the latest trends in streaming, groundbreaking content, and gaming. Our features spotlight the creative minds behind some of the most innovative projects in these fields, offering you exclusive insights into their processes and inspirations. From film festivals to cutting-edge music videos, we celebrate the fusion of artistry and technology that is shaping the future of entertainment.

Our commitment to honoring excellence in the arts continues as we spotlight the stars of FENIX TV and share wisdom from the brightest minds in gaming. This edition is packed with content designed to keep you at the forefront of digital innovation, providing a platform for the pioneers and creators who are pushing the boundaries of what is possible.

Thank you for joining us on this journey of discovery and innovation. As we embrace creativity and explore the future of digital arts and business, we invite you to immerse yourself in the stories and insights within these pages. Together, let's continue to celebrate the innovators who are unveiling the next wave of creativity and technological advancement.

Warm regards,

Adriana Luna Carlos and Hanna Olivas
Editors of FENIX Innovation Magazine

Empowering Voices Through Intuitive Storytelling

Ruth Fae

Ruth Fae, the founder of Fae Blood Publications, has made a significant impact in the world of storytelling through her unique approach as an Intuitive Writing Coach. Ruth's journey into this realm began in 2021 when a series of synchronicities led her to transition from a career in copywriting to creating Fae Blood Publications. Her passion for helping others find their authentic voices and the courage to share their stories has driven her to guide many individuals in their writing and publishing endeavors.

As a copywriter, Ruth enjoyed assisting business owners in crafting content that authentically represented their brands. However, a personal challenge in early 2020 turned her life upside down and set her on a profound healing journey. During this time, she rediscovered her voice, spirituality, and intuition. This period of self-discovery was pivotal, as it reignited her passion for writing and editing. Simultaneously, she began working with clients to edit their books, which deepened her understanding of the importance of authentic storytelling in both business and personal contexts.

The universe seemed to guide Ruth toward indie publishing, where she found a space that aligned with her passion for writing and her desire to help others tell their stories. She realized that her intuition played a crucial role in her ability to guide authors who had been silenced internally and externally. Ruth's approach to working with authors is deeply intuitive, involving a feeling and knowing that transcends words. This connection allows her to create a safe, non-judgmental space for authors to express their truths and share their stories with confidence.

Creating such a space is essential, especially when dealing with authors who are writing about experiences of grief, loss, abuse, and other trauma-related events. Ruth understands the challenges of being vulnerable and expressing emotions, having faced these difficulties herself. Her personal healing journey and intuitive work have equipped her to support authors in overcoming writing blocks, imposter syndrome, and fears of visibility. Ruth embraces the power of co-creation, reassuring her authors that there is no room for self-judgment or criticism in their collaborative process.

One of the most memorable transformations Ruth has witnessed involved a life coach named Georgie, who struggled with anxiety and stress related to writing. Georgie believed she was terrible at writing due to a negative experience with a high school teacher. Through Ruth's guidance, Georgie gradually built her confidence and trust in her ability to use her voice. With Ruth's encouragement and thoughtful feedback, Georgie overcame her fears and discovered a deep connection with her authentic voice. She went on to write and publish a book about her experience with an eating disorder, inspiring many others in the process.

Ruth's journey in the journalism, copywriting, and publishing industries has not been without its challenges. As a freelance journalist with a young family, she struggled to find time for writing and lacked confidence in pitching to editors. Despite these challenges, she persevered and continued to grow. In copywriting, Ruth rejected the conventional "bro-marketing" and "pain points" approach, instead developing a co-creative copywriting coaching method. Though initially met with skepticism, her intuition and determination led her to success.

The indie and hybrid publishing world, where Ruth now thrives, offers a space of openness and acceptance of the healing power of storytelling. Ruth's dedication to maintaining her values in Fae Blood Publications ensures that the focus remains on the quality of the books she publishes and the fair treatment of her authors. She carefully vets each book and follows her intuition to create a long-lasting and authentic business.

Ruth believes that storytelling has the power to challenge societal systems and create change in the world. Through authentic storytelling, individuals can share their lived experiences, bringing awareness, connection, healing, and inspiration to others. Ruth has worked with authors who use their stories to address issues and call for change in various systems, such as education, health, and justice. These authors share their vulnerable experiences to inspire others and create a platform for societal transformation.

For aspiring authors struggling to find their authentic voices, Ruth offers several pieces of advice. She emphasizes the importance of writing first and editing later, being kind and gentle with oneself, and viewing writing as a form of self-care. She encourages authors to create schedules and rituals that support their writing process, embrace creativity, and celebrate their achievements. Ruth also highlights the power of co-creation and the availability of support within the indie publishing community.

As a certified Youth Mentor, Ruth extends her passion for storytelling to younger generations. Her work with young Australians, as a columnist for "Indigo" magazine and a performing arts reviewer for "Dance Writer," has been instrumental in fostering self-expression in youth. In her current role as a writing coach and facilitator of the "Authors Club" at E-Gen, a local homeschooling community, Ruth creates a safe space for young people to explore and express their creativity freely. Her desire to combine her love of writing with mentoring the youth has led to her contribution to the collaborative book "Navigation Tools to Thrive in the Human Experience: A Blueprint for Youth."

Ruth's experience contributing to ten collaborative books has been an enlightening journey. These projects provided her with a safe space to publish her work during her healing process and offered valuable opportunities for networking and building relationships with other authors. Each collaborative book project has taught her different ways of working and reinforced the importance of authenticity in sales and marketing.

Balancing her professional and personal life, especially with a blended family of seven children and a puppy, is a challenge Ruth navigates with a focus on kindness and support. Her family's understanding and help around the home enable her to dedicate time to her work while prioritizing her children's needs. Ruth's partner is supportive and shares the responsibilities of parenting, allowing her to pursue her passion for writing and coaching.

Ruth Fae's dedication to empowering voices through intuitive storytelling has transformed many lives. Her journey, filled with synchronicities and guided by intuition, continues to inspire and support authors in finding and sharing their authentic voices with the world.

ABOUT RUTH:

Founder of Fae Blood Publications, Ruth Fae is an Intuitive Writing Coach, Editor, Publisher, and Author, who helps silenced voices be healed and heard through the powerful, timeless, and magical art of storytelling. In a safe and non-judgemental space, she guides aspiring and established authors to align with their authentic voice and confidently release their stories to the world.

Through her years working in the journalism, copywriting, and publishing industries, Ruth has seen the transformation that can occur when people are truly seen and heard. A rebel at heart, she embodies the belief that we can challenge the systems we live in and create change in the world through sharing our stories and speaking our truth. An avid lover of the performing arts, she is also a certified Youth Mentor who has a keen interest in encouraging the voices and self-expression of our younger generations.

To date, Ruth has been published in ten diverse collaborative books, and loves to explore the many facets of writing, publishing, parenting, and spirituality as a podcast guest and as a writer on Medium.

Residing in Bayside Melbourne, Australia, Ruth Fae shares her 'Life of Love and Magic' with her partner, their blended family of seven children, and an adorably naughty puppy named Merlin.

CONNECT WITH RUTH

🌐 *ruthfaewriter.com*

🌐 *www.faebloodpublications.com*

f *www.facebook.com/faebloodpublications*

📷 *www.instagram.com/fae_blood_publications*

in *www.linkedin.com/in/ruth-fae-writer*

♪ *@ruthfaewriter*

FENIX TV

PREMIER GIFTING LOUNGE IS HEADED TO

EMMYS WEEK

September 9th - 16th, 2024

SHE RISES
STUDIOS

Jamie O'Neill

THE VISIONARY BEHIND SKULL SUGAR COSMETICS

Jamie O'Neill, the innovative mind behind Skull Sugar Cosmetics, has reshaped the beauty industry with her unique blend of creativity, inclusivity, and bold aesthetics. Born and raised in a small town, Jamie's journey to becoming a prominent figure in the cosmetics world is both inspiring and a testament to her determination and vision.

EARLY LIFE AND INSPIRATION

Jamie O'Neill's fascination with makeup began in her teenage years. Growing up, she was captivated by the transformative power of cosmetics, seeing it as an art form that allowed individuals to express their identities and emotions. Her desire to challenge conventional beauty norms led her to establish Skull Sugar Cosmetics in 2013, aiming to create a brand that celebrated diversity and individuality.

KEY MOMENTS: FASHIONXT AND BEYOND

Jamie O'Neill made significant waves in the industry as the key makeup artist backstage at FashioNXT, a prestigious fashion event showcasing cutting-edge designs. Her creative vision and impeccable artistry earned her acclaim, solidifying her reputation as a trailblazer in the makeup world. Working closely with renowned fashion designers, Jamie's work at FashioNXT became synonymous with pushing boundaries and setting trends.

FEATURES IN FORBES & PRESTIGIOUS PUBLICATIONS

Jamie O'Neill's impact extended beyond the runway, gaining recognition in esteemed publications such as Forbes New York and Forbes England. These features highlighted Jamie's entrepreneurial spirit and her dedication to promoting inclusivity in beauty. Her insights into the industry's evolution and her advocacy for diversity resonated deeply, further establishing her as a thought leader. Additionally, Skull Sugar Cosmetics has been prominently featured in various influential magazines, including Natural Health, Gothic Beauty, Harpers Bazaar, and Cosmopolitan. Each feature underscored the brand's commitment to quality and innovation, showcasing its range of products that cater to diverse tastes and preferences.

SKULL SUGAR COSMETICS: EMPOWERING THROUGH BEAUTY

At the core of Skull Sugar Cosmetics lies a commitment to empowering individuals through makeup. The brand's motto, "Beauty for Every Soul," reflects Jamie O'Neill's belief that beauty should be inclusive and accessible to all. From its inception, Skull Sugar has championed diversity, offering a wide array of products designed to complement every skin tone and gender identity. The brand's product lineup is a testament to Jamie's creativity and dedication to excellence. From eyeshadows featuring vibrant and daring shades, to the luxurious "Diva Lacquers" collection known for its rich pigments and long-lasting formulas, each product is crafted with meticulous attention to detail and innovation.

COMMUNITY AND IMPACT

Jamie O'Neill has always prioritized building a strong and supportive community around her brand. Skull Sugar Cosmetics frequently collaborates with influencers, artists, and activists who share the brand's values. These partnerships not only amplify the brand's message but also create a platform for underrepresented voices in the beauty industry. Skull Sugar Cosmetics products are proudly cruelty-free, reflecting Jamie's dedication to creating a positive impact on the world. This ethical stance has resonated with many consumers who are increasingly mindful of the environmental and ethical implications of their purchases.

FUTURE VISION

Looking ahead, Jamie O'Neill has ambitious plans for Skull Sugar Cosmetics. She aims to expand the brand's product line further, exploring new and innovative formulations. Additionally, Jamie is passionate about continuing to use her platform to advocate for diversity and inclusivity in the beauty industry. Jamie O'Neill's journey from a small-town dreamer to the founder of a groundbreaking cosmetics brand is a powerful reminder of what can be achieved with passion, creativity, and a commitment to positive change. Skull Sugar Cosmetics stands as a beacon of inclusivity and self-expression, encouraging everyone to embrace their unique beauty and boldly express themselves.

 WWW.SKULLSUGARCOSMETICS.COM   SKULLSUGARCOSMETICS   JAMIE O'NEILL

SEPTEMBER 13, 2024

HANNA OLIVAS
CHIEF BRANDING OFFICER
SRS STUDIOS & FENIX TV

FENIX TV EMMYS WEEK

PREMIER GIFTING
Suite

OFFICIAL SPONSORS

KIM BEAM

 CORBO COLLECTION   RĒJINS™

Embracing Resilience:
MY JOURNEY FROM ASSAULT TO AUDACITY

My name is Michele Paiva; I am autistic (she/her) and a therapist --and like many readers; I am a survivor of assault, neglect, abuse and loss. Like many readers, I also had the audacity to heal. It's a process and path I am still on.

My journey into the world of financial therapy is deeply intertwined with professional and, my personal experiences.

Before facing significant adversity, my life, like many others, had its share of trials and triumphs. In my early twenties, I was filled with hope and ambition, but a traumatic event would soon alter the course of my life.

I was (sexually) assaulted, left for dead, and underwent emergency surgery to save my life. This harrowing experience shattered me physically, emotionally and financially. I didn't realize then that trauma could have such a profound impact on one's economic well-being.

The Challenge

The trauma I endured left me not only emotionally scarred but financially devastated. The financial strain, coupled with the physical healing, scars that were a reminder and the emotional aftermath, was overwhelming. I was broken in ways I never anticipated, struggling to piece my life back together.

A decade later, my world was further upended when I held my mother, my best friend, as she succumbed to cancer. I had to find the strength to tell her it was okay to let go of her suffering. This moment of profound grief and responsibility was the hardest thing I've ever faced, but it also became a pivotal point in my life.

The Turning Point

The passing of my mother and the profound challenges I faced catalyzed a profound shift in my perspective.

I realized that I didn't want others to endure the silent suffering I experienced or to face financial hardship without understanding the connection between trauma and finances.

This realization was the spark that ignited my transformation. I decided to channel my experiences into something meaningful, leading me to pursue a path in financial therapy.

So much about women is taboo; we are often taught that it isn't ladylike to talk about menstruation, menopause, our assaults or struggles, including financial struggles.

Actions Taken

To address and overcome my challenges, I embarked on a journey of healing and self-discovery. Part of that was being my authentic self; letting my autism be unmasked. Not trying to fit in. It was liberating and I think everyone should let their weird fly as much as possible.

I pursued transpersonal psychology, which combines spiritual and psychological insights, to understand and address the trauma that had impacted my life and finances as well as other women.

I had a career that taught me how women hold so much inside, and suffer in silence. I immersed myself in studying financial literacy and therapy, driven by a desire to help others who faced similar struggles. I wrote three books on financial therapy, sharing my insights and experiences. Additionally, I created the first and only financial therapy app, aiming to provide a unique resource for those seeking to navigate their financial and emotional challenges.

Lessons Learned

My journey taught me that resilience and recovery are not just about overcoming adversity but also about understanding and addressing the underlying issues.

I learned that trauma can profoundly affect financial stability and that healing involves both emotional and practical strategies.

Overcoming these challenges changed me deeply, shaping my approach as a therapist and my commitment to supporting others.

One of the most important lessons is that healing is a spectrum; we may not all be on the autism spectrum, but we are all on a spectrum of healing and overcoming.

Even my physical scars are gone; I was told I would never have children but I did have two. I needed a C-section with my first. My scars were gone because a wonderful OB/GYN when I had that surgical birth, with my daughter, cut the scars away; I didn't know until I woke up that she did this for me.

She had the audacity to heal parts of me that were holding me back, beyond my control- but within hers; and I am forever grateful.

I learned to let go, and use that space as a pivot to create meaningful change, after many tears of course- and sometimes those tears of loss still leak-- but they water and nourish my mission.

Advice for Others

For those facing similar challenges, remember that your journey is unique, and healing takes time. Seek support from professionals who understand the intersection of trauma and financial struggles. Embrace resources and strategies that resonate with you, whether it's therapy, financial education, or self-care practices. Most importantly, be kind to yourself

and acknowledge your progress, no matter how small. While I do not wish pain on anyone, if you have it, remember it is an energy and energy can change form. You are more powerful than you can imagine.

Achieving Success

Today, I am proud of the successes I've achieved despite the obstacles I faced. I think my late mother would be proud of me. It is a homage to her. My work as a financial therapist has allowed me to help others understand and overcome their financial and emotional difficulties. The creation of my app and my books are testaments to the power of resilience and the importance of addressing trauma's impact on financial health. My experiences have fueled my passion for helping others, and I continue to thrive by focusing on my mission to support those in need. Don't be shy about your success. You were meant for greatness.

Future Goals

I expect life will get tough and knock me down a few times; but looking ahead, I aspire to expand my reach and impact through continued innovation in financial therapy. I aim to further develop resources that support individuals in navigating their financial and emotional landscapes. My goal is to inspire and empower more people to find their path to emotional healing and financial stability.

To anyone facing their own challenges, I encourage you to reflect on your journey and seek the support you need. Embrace the lessons you learn along the way and remember that your resilience is a powerful force. Take the first step toward overcoming your obstacles and building a future where you can thrive. Your story is unique, and with the right support and mindset, you can turn assaults to your mind or body into an audacious comeback. Feel free to connect with me at TheFinanceTherapist.com

I am an autistic psychotherapist (she/her) who specializes in financial therapy and trauma. I am far-too fond of 80's sitcoms, watercolor painting, tofu and raising monarch butterflies for release in my spare time.

"Nate and his wife run a very customer-friendly business. When they say, 'Where Service is More than a Transaction,' they really mean it."

"All services they offered are all beyond my expectations."

Photographer Credit: Heidi Schimnich

NATE MAENDEL "THE TREE SURGEON"

With over 30 years of expertise, we specialize in tree removal, trimming, and total property transformations. Year-round tree work, free estimates, and a passion for serving our community make us your go-to for a beautiful, safe outdoor space.

CALL NATE AND OUR NPM TEAM TO THE RESCUE!

218 - 831 - 1142
218 - 831 - 1145

Nate's Property
MAINTENANCE LLC

WHERE SERVICE IS MORE THAN A TRANSACTION

JOIN OUR COMMUNITY

We believe the future is female and that we are better and stronger together. This group is NOT just for entrepreneurs but for women in general of all ages and from all walks of life.

www.bit.ly/srscommunitygroup

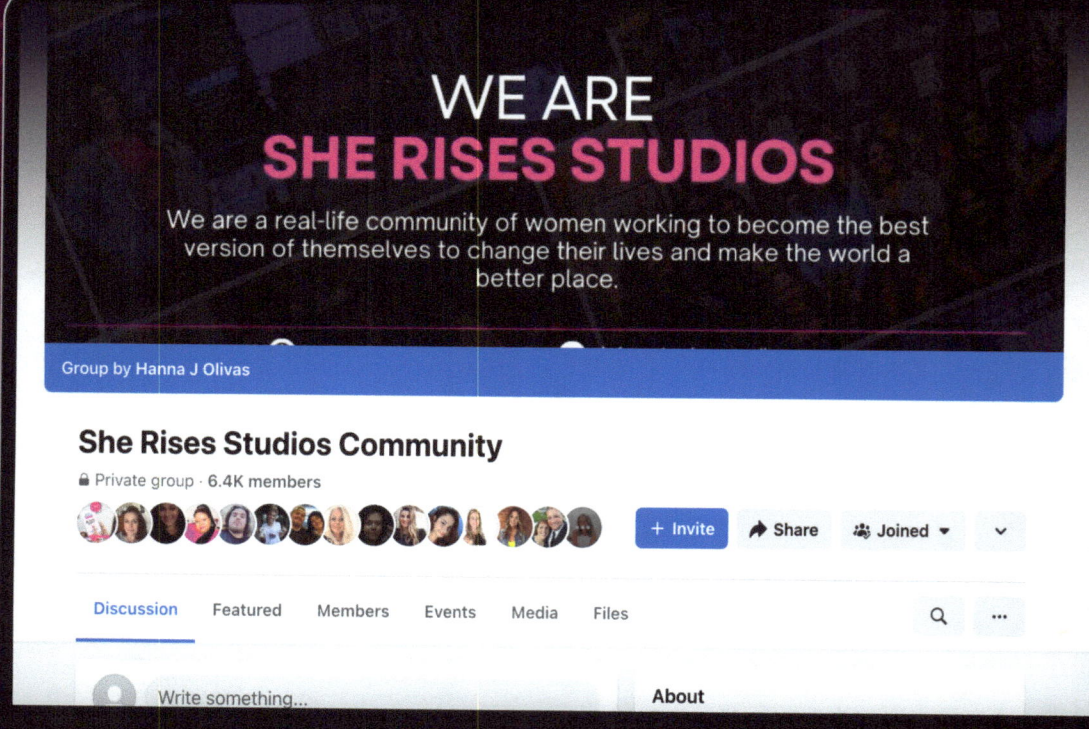

WE ARE
SHE RISES STUDIOS

We are a real-life community of women working to become the best version of themselves to change their lives and make the world a better place.

Group by Hanna J Olivas

She Rises Studios Community

🔒 Private group · 6.4K members

+ Invite   Share   Joined ▾   ˅

Discussion   Featured   Members   Events   Media   Files

Write something...   About

An Immigrant Nightmare Turned into the American Dream

Personal Journey

Background: I'm Arianny Mercedes, an immigrant from the Dominican Republic. My early life was marked by significant challenges, including fleeing gun violence and systemic inequalities in my home country with my family. Despite these hardships, I excelled academically and graduated at the top of my high school class. However, at 18, I faced a significant setback when my scholarship was revoked due to my country of origin, despite being assured of a full ride. This setback was especially disheartening because it felt like my hard work had amounted to nothing.

The Challenge: The revocation of my scholarship was a profound personal and professional challenge. It left me feeling worthless and disillusioned as if my efforts had been in vain. The impact was not just emotional but also financial, as I had to navigate a new path under challenging circumstances. Either I went into over $150K in debt for an undergraduate degree or sucked up my ego and attended community college. I decided my ego was not that strong, so I attended community college.

The Turning Point

Defining Moment: The turning point came when I started working as a hostess at a high-end steakhouse. A regular guest, recognizing my potential, suggested I explore a career in human resources. This unexpected encouragement was the catalyst that sparked a change in my approach and mindset. He shared his business card with me and suggested I follow up.

Actions Taken: Embracing this new direction, I reached out to him. Long story, short, while still attending community college I was able to land a full-time role to help me afford my studies. I transitioned into human resources, which led to a successful career. I leveraged every opportunity to learn and grow, ultimately founding my own career and workplace consulting firm, Revamped.

I relied on mentorship, continuous learning, and my growing network to navigate and overcome the challenges I faced.

Lesson Learned

Key Takeaways: The most important lesson I learned is that setbacks can be redirections rather than dead ends. Overcoming adversity taught me resilience, adaptability, and the value of unexpected opportunities. These experiences have shaped me into a more determined and resourceful professional.

Advice for Others: For those facing similar challenges, my advice is to remain open to unexpected opportunities and seek support from mentors and peers. Embrace setbacks as learning experiences and use them as fuel for your journey forward. Persistence and adaptability are key to overcoming obstacles.

Achieving Success

Current Achievements: Today, I am the founder of Revamped, a workplace consulting firm that has helped over 500 professionals. Additionally, I provide over 100K global followers with free resources, insights, remote job postings, and motivation to help them alongside their career strides.

My book of total client salaries exceeds $10M, and I have accumulated over 7 years of HR experience. I also graduated from the University of Virginia with honors graduating debt-free and have worked with leading organizations like American Express and Accenture. These achievements are a testament to the resilience and determination that emerged from my early challenges.

My words and insights have been tapped by leading publications like US World News, Business Insider, CNN, and NPR. I've spoken on panels at Columbia Business School and conferences sponsored by leading tech companies including Google and Microsoft.

Future Goals: Looking ahead, I plan to continue expanding Revamped, helping more professionals achieve their career goals, and contributing positively to the workplace consulting industry. My vision is to inspire and support others in their professional journeys, making a lasting impact on their lives and careers.

I am also studying for the LSAT and GRE to embark on a path towards a JD/MBA as I aspire to transform my consultancy to offer legal council while mastering the essence of building a sustainable business.

Inspiring Others: Be delusional. Believe in your wildest dreams. I encourage people, especially women from underserved communities to reflect on their own challenges and view them as opportunities for growth. No will always mean no if you let it.

Take the first step towards overcoming obstacles by embracing new opportunities and seeking support. Remember, resilience and a positive mindset can transform setbacks into powerful catalysts for success.

Website: www.ariannymercedes.com

Instagram: www.instagram.com/ariannymercedess

Twitter: www.x.com/ariannnyy

LinkedIn: www.linkedin.com/in/arianny

AUTHOR
Spotlights

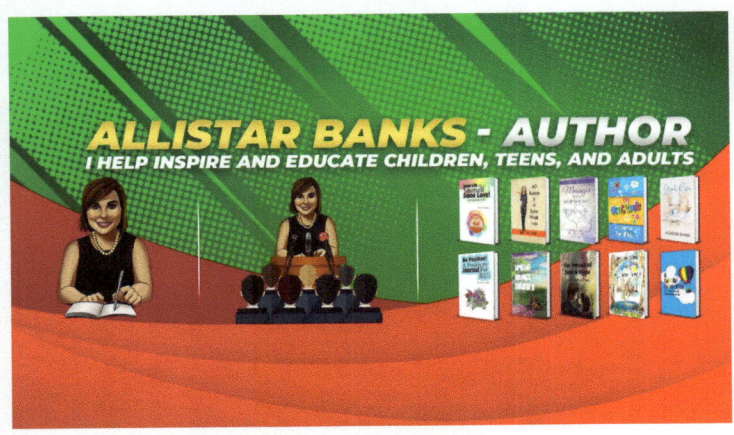

EXPLORING THE DIVERSE WORLD OF A MULTI-GENRE AUTHOR

In the realm of literature, there exist authors whose creative genius transcends the boundaries of traditional genres. Allistar Banks, a multi-genre author of children's books, teen books, and adult books has effortlessly navigated through various literary styles, weaving compelling narratives that captivate readers across different genres. Her titled books are A Colorful Balloon Ride, Lenny the Lizard and His Green Scarf, Spring Brings Summer, The Pursuit of Love & Hope A Short Collection of Poems, Girl Rise, her three gratitude journals for all ages, and more.

Allistar Banks has shown her versatile and prolific writing skills through various genres from fun and adventure for children to drama-based books for adults. Whether it is delving into the realm of fun and adventure for children, crafting intricate romantic themes, or exploring the depths of human emotions in poignant literary fiction, this author's body of work showcases a remarkable range of storytelling prowess.

One of the hallmarks of Allistar Banks' writing is The Pursuit of Love & Hope A Short Collection of Poems where she delves into expressing a period of identity crisis and realizing her true self. By infusing her writing with vivid imagery, complex characters, and thought-provoking themes in Girl, Rise where her alter ego Alli Billings struggles with self-worth. She creates immersive worlds that resonate with readers on a deep and emotional level.

In the realm of self-help, Allistar Banks is celebrated for their innovative approach to mental health through her gratitude journals called The Gratitude Journal for Kids, Show Life & Yourself Some Love! A Gratitude Journal for Teens, and Be Positive! A Positivity Journal for Adults. Her journaling techniques help all ages cope with stress and other related mental health challenges.

When it comes to physical health and nutrition, Allistar Banks excels in crafting recipes and keeping readers loving food in 40 Recipes to Tackle Diabetes and 40 Recipes for a Better Weight Loss.

As readers immerse themselves in the diverse world of her books, they are invited on a journey that spans across genres, inviting them to explore new worlds, unravel mysteries, and connect with characters whose stories resonate long after the final page is turned. With each new book, she continues to captivate audiences with their boundless creativity, leaving a lasting impact on the literary landscape.

In conclusion, Allistar Banks stands as a shining example of the boundless creativity and the transformative power of storytelling that can be found in the work of a multi-genre author. Through her expansive body of work, the author invites readers to embrace the beauty of diversity in literature and to celebrate the richness of storytelling in all its forms. In a world where boundaries between genres are blurred, Allistar stands as a beacon of inspiration for writers and readers alike, showcasing the endless possibilities that come with embracing the art of storytelling in its many shapes and forms.

www.Facebook.com/AllistarAuthor   www.Instagram.com/allistarthewriter   www.tiktok.com/@allistarthewriter

UNSTOPPABLE WOMAN DARES EXECUTIVES TO LEAD WITH A FIERCE HEART

by Merilee Kern, MBA

Relational leadership and management authority Cheryl L. Mason, J.D. is a force of nature. TEDx speaker, author and CEO, Mason his hell bent on helping C-suite executives, senior leaders, companies, and teams develop the skills and tools to lead with authenticity and empathy. As the fourth Presidentially-appointed, Senate-confirmed—and first woman and military spouse—to serve as the CEO/Chairman of the VA Board of Veterans' Appeals prior to starting her own Catalyst Leadership Management business consultancy, Mason is revered for leading with an impactful morale-boosting, people-centric approach—and teaching other managers how to do the same.

Mason brings a unique perspective on adversity and challenges by viewing them as pivotal moments for learning and growth. Additionally, she addresses and highlights the negative impact of invisible "phantom" leaders on the people and the organization. Her consultancy services help CEOs, senior leaders, companies, and teams develop the skills and tools to lead with authenticity and relate with empathy. Mason's mission is to help other business leaders discover and embrace the power of authenticity—being real, caring, relatable, accessible and engaging with each leader's most valuable asset: the people they lead and impact.

As an author and a TEDx speaker, Mason shares insights and stories about people, obstacles, purpose, impact and mindset along with tactical ways leaders can elevate results. Mason is more than a speaker; she's a dynamic force of nature. Her captivating keynote presentations have graced the TEDx stage and have left a profound mark on corporations and nonprofits alike. With her wealth of knowledge, real-world experience, and infectious enthusiasm for leadership, Mason has inspired countless individuals to reach their full potential and take their leadership skills to new heights. She shares her inspiring journey of overcoming life's challenges, while seamlessly incorporating valuable lessons on leadership, vulnerability, and courage. Her ability to connect with business and corporate audiences leaves a lasting impact, empowering others to face adversity with resilience and determination.

Merilee Kern, MBA is an internationally-regarded brand strategist and analyst who reports on noteworthy industry change makers, movers, shakers and innovators across all B2B and B2C categories. Connect with her at LinkedIn www.LinkedIn.com/in/MerileeKern.

In her book, "Dare to Relate: Leading with a Fierce Heart," which emphasizes the significance of cultivating strong relationships within your workforce, Mason shares her journey and unveils her unconventional, yet highly effective approach to leadership.

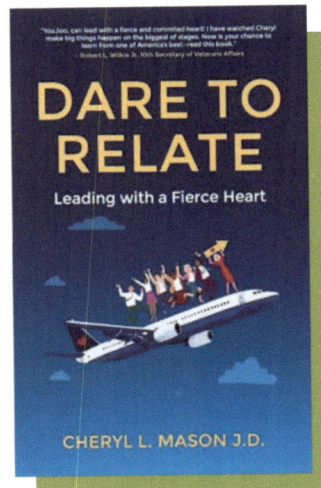

The book highlights how investing time, technology and finances into the employee pool can spur long-term savings substantial bottom line results. The book highlights how relational leadership enhances staff well-being and drives success for leaders and their organizations at large. Through relatable personal stories and insights from her network, Mason's book not only encourages and guides aspirationals to find their own inner leader, but also emphasizes the importance of purposefully impacting the world today and tomorrow.

Mason realized an exceptional career at the Department of Veterans Affairs, beginning as a young attorney and climbing the ranks to eventually become the first woman and military spouse—and senate confirmed—Chairman of the Board of Veterans' Appeals. As the CEO leading over 1200 people serving the veteran and stakeholder communities, she implemented technological innovations to benefit both her employees and customers. Through collaboration with her team, she achieved remarkable results, doubling customer outcomes and increasing morale, retention, and trust. Mason not only successfully grew and managed a large budget but also built and led the most diverse team of people in our history.

With over 30 years of dedicated federal service, coupled with her role as a USAF military spouse, Mason held various challenging positions in the legal and administrative domains. Her accomplishments include establishing an educational program for service members and their families in Germany, managing a diverse range of USAFE support programs encompassing contracts, personnel, budget, and IT, and spearheading a large-scale complex legal operation at the Department of Veterans Affairs (VA). Throughout her career, she has earned a well-deserved reputation as an inspiring leader, placing utmost importance on her team, their families, and the successful accomplishment of their mission.

As Chairman of the Board of Veterans' Appeals at the VA, she led a team of 1200 personnel, including veterans law judges, attorneys, and operations and administrative professionals, and executed a budget of $228 million to meet the Board's mission of conducting hearings and deciding appeals on benefits and services for veterans and their families. As a principal, she advised the Secretary of the VA on diverse matters, from wide-ranging veterans' issues to stakeholder concerns. She implemented revolutionary technological innovations, streamlined processes, and created cost-saving solutions. She improved operations by creating consistency in management practices and championed the investment in personnel by securing more than 65 percent in budget increases over 4 years. She is credited with turning the Board from a dysfunctional organization with low morale and trust and lackluster results into a high-functioning organization, delivering results to veterans and increasing trust and morale in her employees through her people-focused leadership style.

Mason served as Interim Principal Deputy Vice Chairman at the Board of Veterans' Appeals where she was responsible for legislation, regulation, and policy, which included building a diverse political alliance to build consensus with VA leadership, stakeholders and Congress to gain passage of the Veterans Appeals Improvement and Modernization Act of 2017.

Additionally, Mason held a variety of positions, including Deputy Vice Chairman and Veterans Law Judge at the Board, attorney with the Federal Labor Relations Authority, and a Department of the Air Force civilian at HQ United States Air Forces in Europe at Ramstein Air Base, Germany. Mason also served as a contract attorney investigator for the Department of Justice Civil Rights Division specializing in the Americans with Disabilities Act; a military services paralegal coordinator for Europe with Central Texas College; and an instructor at Central Texas College, Kapaun Air Station, Germany.

She also served as a PREVENTS Task Force Ambassador, along with Lead Ambassador Second Lady Karen Pence. PREVENTS was the first national public health campaign to address suicide prevention. Mason also worked closely with First Lady Dr. Jill Biden's Joining Forces initiative to address the challenges and issues of military and veteran families.

In recognition of her fierce commitment and actions around military spouse employment and transitioning veterans, Mason received the Hiring Our Heroes 2022 Bonnie Amos Lifetime Achievement Impact Award from the US Chamber of Commerce. Mason was recognized by Disabled American Veterans as the 2021 Outstanding Federal Executive and received the FedHealthIT 2020 Leading for Impact: Women in Leadership Award.

Mason's extraordinary journey stands as a testament to her unwavering dedication and exceptional leadership prowess. Being a catalyst leader involves facing challenges, overcoming obstacles, and genuinely caring for and supporting your employees.

A Haunting with a Twist

Who would build a house purposely to be haunted?

100 people have perished or gone missing over three decades. Now two paranormal research teams enter to solve the mystery. But first they must learn to work together if they want to survive Blood Mansion.

"I did enjoy it -- especially after they all got to the house. I thought there was good tension and I found it rather spooky -- or at least as spooky as someone like me could find that sort of story. But, yeah, I was into it and rooting for the good guys!

I did smile a few times at the skeptical investigators and recognized some of our attitudes and techniques. Other times I thought to myself, 'If we'd seen that, I might have a different attitude!'"

James Underdown
Renowned Paranormal Investigator

"Wow! 'Blood Mansion' is an electrifying journey through the shadows of destiny and the complexities of morality."

Kate Milly
May 12, 2024

 www.storywriter.ca

From Diagnosis to the Red Carpet:

Hanna Olivas, Chief Branding Officer of She Rises Studios and FENIX TV, Proves Dreams Have No Limits

Hanna Olivas, the powerhouse Chief Branding Officer of She Rises Studios and FENIX TV, is set to make a grand entrance on the red carpet at this year's Emmy Awards, where she will also host the prestigious FENIX TV Premier Gifting Suite for Emmys week. Hanna's journey is a testament to the unyielding spirit of resilience, having turned a terminal diagnosis of rare blood cancer, multiple myeloma, into a mission to inspire women worldwide.

Hanna Olivas's story is one of extraordinary courage and unwavering determination. When diagnosed with multiple myeloma, Hanna chose not to let the terminal illness define her life. Instead, she channeled her will to live into creating She Rises Studios, a groundbreaking platform dedicated to empowering women entrepreneurs, and FENIX TV, an innovative online streaming service.

"Facing a terminal diagnosis made me realize that every moment is precious," said Hanna Olivas. "I wanted to leave a legacy that would inspire women to pursue their dreams, no matter the obstacles."

Hanna's efforts have not gone unnoticed. She has been featured in hundreds of media appearances, including the Today Show, Tamron Hall, People Magazine, and more. Her compelling story and magnetic presence have made her a beacon of hope for countless women striving to overcome their own challenges.

This year, Hanna's journey comes full circle as she walks the red carpet at the Emmys, a symbol of her triumph over adversity. Hosting the FENIX TV Emmys Gifting Suite in Beverly Hills, she brings together Hollywood's elite to celebrate not only the industry's best but also the indomitable human spirit.

Hanna Olivas is a shining example of how dreams can come true regardless of the hurdles life throws at us," said Hanna Olivas, CEO of She Rises Studios. "Her story is an inspiration to all, showing that with passion and perseverance, anything is possible."

Hanna's mission goes beyond business success. Through She Rises Studios and FENIX TV, she aims to create a supportive community for women, providing the resources and encouragement they need to succeed in their entrepreneurial endeavors.

As Hanna graces the Emmy Awards red carpet and hosts the FENIX TV Emmys Gifting Suite, she stands as a living testament to the power of resilience, determination, and the unwavering belief that no diagnosis can define one's destiny.

About She Rises Studios

She Rises Studios is a leading platform dedicated to empowering women entrepreneurs through resources, education, and community support. Founded by Hanna Olivas, the studio aims to inspire and elevate women to achieve their fullest potential.

FENIX TV is an innovative online streaming platform that showcases a diverse array of content, focusing on empowerment, inspiration, and education. It is committed to providing a platform for voices that deserve to be heard and stories that need to be told.

About FENIX TV

Hanna Olivas's journey is a powerful reminder that dreams are achievable, no matter the challenges faced along the way. Her story continues to inspire and uplift women around the world, proving that with grit and determination, anything is possible!

www.facebook.com/HannaJOlivas
www.sherisesstudios.com
www.instagram.com/hannaolivasofficial
www.youtube.com/@SheRIsesStudios
www.tiktok.com/@sherisesstudios
www.linkedin.com/in/hanna-olivas-93baa617a

RISING STRONG:
My Journey from Survival to Success

My name is Jennifer Johnson and I am the owner of True Fashionistas, the largest lifestyle resale store in Florida.

I grew up on a farm in central Minnesota the 2nd oldest of 6 siblings. My dad showed me and my siblings what hard work was like. He worked tirelessly to put food on our table and make ends meet for my family.

My last year in high school I met a boy whom I began dating. He seemed great at first until he started hitting me, abusing me verbally. I didn't know that the hitting and verbal abuse would be the least of my issues. The physical violence turned into sexual violence with him raping me. I didn't matter that I said no he would continue each and every time. The violence also got worse. It got so bad that when I graduated and was going on to college on a scholarship for broadcast communications (I wanted to be a TV news anchor so bad) he threatened to kill me if I ended up going. I never went to college because I was so scared.

The turning point was one night he drove me off the road and tried to kill me. Something changed in me that night. Something just clicked and I realized this is not how I want to live my life. I feel it was as though God was talking to me saying get out now while you are still alive. It was by that grace of God that I did get out. Over the course of the next few months I was able to distance myself from him, get a restraining order and take my life back. This was something I really did on my own because I didn't want anyone to think less of me or not believe me. It was a very tough time but I drew on my faith (even though I didn't understand it at the time) to get me through.

This entire experience changed me. At the time I thought it was terrible, and it was, but now 30+ years later reflecting on this entire experience I learned so much about myself and about resilience. Your past becomes part of the fabric that you are today. You use your past to change you future and to make your future even better.

I realize that no matter what you are facing there will be light at the end of the tunnel and things in life happen FOR you not TO you! The reason all of this happened to me was so that now, later in life, I am able to go out and speak to people and motivate them and I do just that. From small stages to large stages to intimate events. I speak about what happened to me, how I got out and what I am doing with what happened to me now. f I can help just ONE person then what I went through was all worth it.

I harnessed all that negativity, violence and pain and went on to become Ms. Petite MN, a model and actress and advocate for stopping sexual violence.

I am now an entrepreneur (I owe 3 different companies) as well as an author, small business coach and professional speaker. I use all that life has thrown at me and use it to encourage others.

My goal is to continue speaking in front of audiences world wide to spread the voice of encouragement, resilience and hope.

I invite each of you to look at your own life and the challenges that you have faced along the way. What have they taught you? What were the lessons, as there always lessons in everything that happens for us. It is our job to find out what those lessons are, learn from them and teach them to others so it can better their lives.

I didn't allow the challenges of my past to hold me down. I took the challenges of my past and harnessed them to create a better future for myself I used them to propel me to become UNSTOPPABLE!

Jennifer Ann Johnson

From national model to founder of a successful resale empire, Jennifer Johnson embodies entrepreneurial grit and grace. As the visionary behind True Fashionistas, Florida's largest lifestyle resale store, she's mastered building a thriving business while maintaining personal well-being. Her Amazon bestseller and award-winning podcast offer a blueprint for success that resonates with business owners everywhere.

Jennifer's impact extends far beyond her own achievements. As a coach and speaker, she's transformed countless entrepreneurs' lives through her online academy and coaching programs. Her expertise, featured in Forbes and Vogue, coupled with her dynamic presence from national TV appearances, captivates and inspires action.

Recognized as a Gulfshore Life Businesswoman of the Year, Jennifer doesn't just teach success – she embodies it. Her blend of experience, strategies, and motivational energy empowers audiences to achieve their dreams.

Facebook: www.facebook.com/profile.php?id=100089312054101&mibextid=LQQJ4d
Instagram: Jennifer.ann_johnson
Linkedin: www.linkedin.com/in/jennifer-johnson-39237448/
True FashionistasFacebook: www.facebook.com/truefashionistasresale/
Instagram: truefashionistasresale

FROM MUMBAI TO MILLIONAIRE: MY JOURNEY OF RESILIENCE AND REINVENTION

Growing up in Mumbai, India, I was immersed in the city's relentless hustle and vibrant vitality. My parents' sacrifices were the foundation of my aspirations, as I was raised in a middle-class family. Their unwavering support enabled me to relocate to the United States in order to pursue my aspiration of establishing my own business and pursuing higher education. I was aware that I required a distinct environment to transform my entrepreneurial aspirations into a reality after encountering the bureaucratic and unethical practices in India.

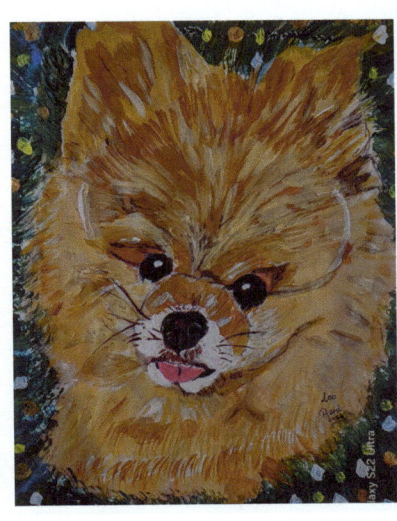

The year 2010 marked a significant turning point in my existence. I held a secure position as the Vice President of Product Management at a major corporation, and my wife and I were expecting our first child. My wife encouraged me to establish my own business, as she was aware that if I did not act now, I may never achieve it. I established my company with her assistance, motivated by pioneering concepts regarding video interview technology that were ahead of their time.

The initial year was exceedingly difficult. Due to my existing connections, acquiring my initial client was relatively straightforward; however, attracting subsequent clients proved to be a more challenging endeavor. I experienced a decline in my professional identity as I transitioned from the role of VP of Product Management to that of a recruiter. I found this change to be difficult to accept, and I encountered difficulties with the brand's perception. At times, I entertained the idea of resigning and returning to my corporate career.

The pivotal moment occurred when I elected to collaborate with a coach who introduced me to the concept of "burning the bridge," which involved eliminating the safety net that bound me to my previous identity. My perspective changed as soon as I relinquished that rope. I accepted my new position and concentrated on becoming the most effective recruiter possible. My company experienced accelerated growth as a result of our ability to differentiate our services and refine our business practices. We achieved a $1 million revenue within three years, and by 2015, we had multiplied it.

The oil and gas industry experienced a subsequent collapse, which resulted in numerous companies losing their footing. We reacted to the downturn by pivoting. Our revenue increased by another million as we examined new industries and established a consulting division. Our capacity to pivot and adapt became our most significant asset, enabling us to persist in our growth despite the obstacles.

My personal and professional life have been significantly altered as a result of my ability to surmount these challenges. I have acquired an understanding of the significance of adaptability, resilience, and the ability to embrace change. Burning the bridge was an essential lesson that compelled me to perpetually innovate and commit fully.

I recommend that those who are confronted with comparable obstacles embrace change and relinquish the safety nets that constrain them. Obtain assistance from mentors or coaches and concentrate on setting yourself apart in your profession. Your greatest allies are adaptability and resilience. No matter how insurmountable the challenges may appear, have faith in your capacity to adapt and develop.

Presently, the following accomplishments have: My company is currently flourishing, and our transition from a small startup to a multi-million-dollar enterprise is a testament to our innovation and resilience. Our success has been significantly influenced by our capacity to pivot, and we have established a reputation for excellence in our field.

I aspire to continue to have a positive influence in the future. I intend to broaden our offerings, investigate new markets, and enhance our innovation. In addition to my professional pursuits, I derive satisfaction and significance from contributing to others. Painting portraits of deceased canines is one method I employ to provide solace to their families. This practice is soul-nourishing, bringing pleasure to others and providing me with a sense of fulfillment.

Consider your obstacles and determine how you can incorporate these teachings into your personal life. Embrace change, seek assistance, and do not hesitate to destroy the bridge that hinders your progress. Begin the process of surmounting your challenges and achieving an unstoppable status. Incredible success and growth can result from your voyage, regardless of its challenges.

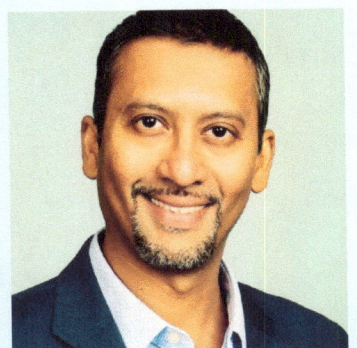

ABHIJEET NARVEKAR

Abhi, originally from Mumbai, moved to the USA for his Master's in Industrial Engineering. In 2010, he founded his company, which has been recognized as one of the Fastest Growing Alumni companies from Oklahoma State University and has won multiple Best Places to Work awards. Passionate about helping others, Abhi's impact is captured in testimonials like, "Abhi changed my life!" His dedication to creating a supportive and dynamic workplace is the cornerstone of his success.

www.thefervidgroup.com
www.careerunleashed.com
www.linkedin.com/in/abhijeetnarvekar

FENIX TV

SHE RISES STUDIOS

EMPOWER**HER** CONTENT DAY

at

Elevate Your Brand Through Creative And Impactful Content!

EmpowerHer Content Day equips attendees with the tools and knowledge needed to craft compelling content for social media, podcasts, and videos.

FEBRUARY 22, 2025

TOTAL ACCESS TICKET: $127

WWW.SHERISESSTUDIOS.COM

by Ashleigh Netter

BETTING ON YOURSELF: NAVIGATING LIFE'S STORMS FOR AUTHENTIC SUCCESS

Imagine having everything in place: a stable job, a supportive family, and a bright future. Now imagine losing all of that within 24 hours. How would you feel? Devastated? Confused? Angry? Afraid?

I've felt all of these emotions, but most of all, I've felt numb. Life's storms—whether personal, professional, or environmental—can dismantle everything we've worked for in an instant.

For me, it was on August 29, 2005, when Hurricane Katrina hit New Orleans, Louisiana, with unprecedented force. I went from an aspiring pharmacist student to a survivor navigating the chaos the storm left behind.

The Turning Point

Life's unpredictability shook me to my core, leaving me feeling like I was navigating a storm without a compass. The idea of betting on myself seemed like a gamble, but in this moment it was the most empowering choice I could make. Instead of succumbing to the chaos, I chose to take risks, embrace challenges, and transform my life and career. This encounter sparked the creation of my life's mission: Living to Inspire and Transform (LIT).

Risk #1: GET L.I.T.! I must live to inspire and transform in everything I do.

Embracing Life's Storms

Life's storms bring challenges, but instead of avoiding them, embrace them. Each storm teaches us resilience, determination, big-picture thinking, and emotional intelligence. These qualities become our assets —our capital gains. Embrace your storms, own them, and leverage the lessons they provide.

Principle 1: Embrace the Challenge

Every storm, whether a personal setback, a career obstacle, or a financial crisis, comes with its own set of challenges. Embrace these challenges rather than avoiding them. They teach us resilience, determination, and the ability to see the bigger picture. These qualities become your capital gains—valuable assets that you can leverage for authentic success.

Principle 2: Inspire Through Your Journey

Authentic success isn't just about personal achievement; it's about inspiring others. Listen and reflect before responding. This practice allows you to check your emotional capacity and respond effectively. When you find yourself in others' stories and build genuine connections, you not only inspire hope but also create a supportive network.

Principle 3: Transform with Gratitude

Practice daily gratitude, especially for the storms. Gratitude transforms every area of life, fostering an environment of kindness, respect, and support. This mindset benefits you and those around you, creating a community of growth and support.

Betting on Yourself

Betting on oneself means taking risks and embracing the unknown with confidence. It's about believing in your ability to overcome obstacles and turn challenges into opportunities.

Here's how you can do it:

- **Acknowledge Your Strengths:** Recognize and celebrate your abilities and achievements. This boosts your confidence and prepares you to face new challenges.
- **Set Clear Goals:** Define what success means to you. Set realistic and achievable goals that align with your values and aspirations.
- **Take Calculated Risks:** Step out of your comfort zone and take risks that can lead to growth. Assess the potential outcomes and make informed decisions.
- **Learn from Failures:** View failures as learning opportunities. Analyze what went wrong, learn from it, and apply those lessons to future endeavors.
- **Seek Support:** Surround yourself with supportive individuals who believe in your vision. Their encouragement can provide the motivation needed to keep moving forward.

The Impact of Betting on Yourself

Applying these principles can significantly impact your life and community. Through leadership and influence, you can secure opportunities, create initiatives, and support those in need.

For example, I've been able to secure over $1.5 million in corporate dollars to establish scholarship programs, feed thousands of families, and launch initiatives that provide essential services to underserved communities.

This isn't a flex; it's a testament to what betting on yourself and being L.I.T. can achieve.

My story is a powerful reminder that we all can rise from our personal Katrinas. As you reflect on your life, consider where you can take the risk to bet on yourself. What areas of your life are ripe for change? What dreams have you been putting off because of fear or uncertainty? Now is the time to act. Whether it's starting a new career, launching a business, or pursuing a personal passion, take that leap of faith.

Ask yourself: What do I have to lose? More importantly, what do I have to gain? Success on social media and trending topics often stem from those who dared to bet on themselves. They share their journeys, their failures, and their victories, inspiring others to do the same.

So, share your story. Document your journey. Let your experience inspire others. Use hashtags like #BetOnYourself, #TakeTheRisk, #GetLIT and #AuthenticSuccess to connect with a community of risk-takers and dream-chasers.

My challenge to you is to show up every day betting on yourself. Take risks, embrace your storms, and inspire and transform those around you.

My name is Dr. Ashleigh Netter, and I believe in betting on myself for authentic success. Connect with me on ashleighnetter.com, LinkedIn, Instagram, and YouTube.

by Christina Collura

AUTISM ADVOCACY TO ENTREPRENEURIAL SUCCESS

"If they can't learn the way we teach – maybe we should teach they way we learn".

A quote that I always lived by and it became even more apparent after my son's Autism diagnosis. My name is Christina Collura, I am a mom of two boys, a full-time educator, turned Autism advocate and award-winning entrepreneur. I was married for almost 12 years and in that time, faced the most challenging realization – my youngest son is Autistic. In that time, I was also dealing with Stage 4 endometriosis which required extensive surgery to even be able to tackle the ups and downs with my son's diagnosis and of course, my own life, insecurities and anxiety.

With Luca (my son's) diagnosis came the "AH-HA" moment, and a turning point that went back to the very quote that you read at the beginning. Luca's diagnosis wasn't going to be a barrier, but simply a leaning curve for everyone that he encountered- figuring out how he needed to learn. This completely changed my mentality both professional and personally and made the quote even more blinding!

Luca loved the texture and using chalk as a catalyst for colouring, scribbling etc.He could spend all day scribbling and doodling on my driveway. I decided to put that interest to good use and apply it to a wooden name puzzle. I hand painted a chalkboard base to the indented spaces of the puzzle – and watched his fine motor skills develop – with not being able to go "out of the lines" as he wrote the letters in his name L-u-c-a. 4 weeks later – this spiraled onto paper and my mind was blown! How did I just come up with an idea to help my son to learn to successfully write his name?

I took this idea – literally googled a manufacturer overseas (who turned out to be one of the biggest in China), got a prototype made for and Uppercase and Numbers 1-20 puzzle (with a chalkboard base) and brought the successful concept into my Kindergarten classroom and saw the same success!! The difference was – many other children – both on and off the spectrum – wanted to play!! An inclusive product concept that just brough children of all needs and abilities together!Did I just do this? Facing my own obstacles, demons, fears, I took the idea and ran with it. We are currently a fast-growing brand with a patented concept that is reaching more and more children, while advocating and spreading inclusivity along the way.

Throughout this process, I continue to look back and realize that I am the only one that could have made this happen. People often ask me "how did I get here?".My response is always "one day at a time". That stands true with battling the challenges of Autism everyday! I continue to learn and grow with my son – one day at a time.

Being named Top 100 Inspirational Woman through my work with Autism Awareness, An RBC Woman of Influence Nominee, Mom's Choice Award Winner, Parent's Pick Award Winner, Total Mom Pitch Top 100 (to name a few) – I continue to have pinch me moments – but the reality is – it all comes back to the one decision I made after my son's diagnosis – to figure out how he needed to learn! That was the most important decision I made with that tough diagnosis.

I inspire all woman out there to make the best possible decision for both you and your family. Forget about what everyone else is going to think – and decide your own path and go for it!You'll never be disappointed for trying – you'll be more disappointed for not!

Becoming a successful entrepreneur while raising an autistic child requires resilience, adaptability, and a unique set of skills. Here are some key ideas that I continue to draw upon from such a journey

RESILIENCE AND PERSEVERANCE

- **Never Give Up:** The journey is filled with challenges, from balancing parenting responsibilities with business demands to overcoming societal stigma. Resilience is key.

- **Embrace Failures:** Viewing setbacks as learning opportunities rather than failures can propel growth and improvement.

TIME MANAGEMENT AND PRIORITIZATION

- **Effective Time Management:** Balancing business and personal responsibilities requires meticulous planning and prioritization.
- **Delegation:** Learning to delegate tasks in business and seeking support in parenting (e.g., from family, friends, or professional caregivers) is crucial.

ADAPTABILITY AND FLEXIBILITY

- **Stay Adaptable:** Both business and parenting can be unpredictable. Being flexible and adaptable helps in navigating sudden changes and challenges.
- **Creative Problem-Solving:** Finding creative solutions for both business hurdles and parenting challenges can make a significant difference.

ADVOCACY AND AWARENESS

- **Raise Awareness:** Being an advocate for autism awareness can create a supportive community and potentially open business opportunities.
- **Network and Connect:** Building a strong network of other parents, professionals, and business connections can provide emotional support and practical advice.

SELF-CARE AND MENTAL HEALTH

- **Prioritize Self-Care:** Taking care of oneself is crucial to avoid burnout. This includes finding time for rest, hobbies, and mental health care.
- **Seek Professional Help:** Therapy or counseling can provide support for managing stress and maintaining mental well-being.

FINANCIAL MANAGEMENT

- **Smart Financial Planning:** Careful financial planning and budgeting are essential to manage both business expenses and the costs associated with raising a child with special needs.
- **Seek Funding and Grants:** Exploring available funding, grants, or financial aid for both business and autism-related needs can provide additional support.

EDUCATION AND LEARNING

- **Continuous Learning:** Keeping up with both business trends and the latest in autism research and therapies can provide valuable insights and strategies.
- **Leverage Resources:** Utilizing available resources such as online courses, support groups, and business mentorship programs can aid in personal and professional growth.

EMPATHY AND COMPASSION

- **Empathetic Leadership:** Leading with empathy and understanding can create a positive work environment and build strong relationships with clients and employees.
- **Teaching Inclusivity:** Promoting inclusivity and understanding within the business can set a positive example and create a supportive community.

CELEBRATING SMALL WINS

- **Celebrate Milestones:** Recognizing and celebrating small victories, both in business and personal life, can boost morale and provide motivation to keep going.
- **Practice Gratitude:** Maintaining a positive outlook and practicing gratitude can improve overall well-being and provide a sense of accomplishment.

You really are your own worst critique; but I also know I have one (two) sweet boys that need my drive and dedication! I need it too! You can and will do it – you just need to put your mind to it to become the most "unstoppable" version of yourself!

Christina Collura
Full Time Educator of 20 years
CEO AND FOUNDER – Creative Beginning

www.creativebeginning.ca
www.facebook.com/creativebeginning
www.instagram.com/creativebeginning

by Darlene Taylor

CULTIVATING STRENGTH, SELF-LOVE, AND A PURPOSE-FILLED PATH THROUGH ADVERSITY

Having to endure one life-altering-do-over after another has forged the courage to face whatever comes my way as I know that I have cultivated the strength of character and self-love to weather any storm that may shift its winds my way. Several years ago, I abandoned my career, divorced, and became wholeheartedly focused on my role as a mother. All those life-altering changes sent me on a self-discovery path over the next few years, which morphed into the opportunity of a lifetime to explore and define myself.

MY JOURNEY

I was always a dedicated student to whom academic success was extremely important. I decided to become a therapist at age 14 and never looked back, working hard toward that goal and holding tightly to the idea that a successful career was the most important achievement I could attain. I earned a Master's in Social Work, nurturing a dream to change the world, one family at a time. I focused intently on my career, taking for granted that I would easily fall into the traditional cycle of life - find a husband and have a family.

Naively, I created a plan in my head during graduate school that laid out precisely how adulthood would unfold, but by graduation, I felt behind schedule and pressured to make my current relationship official - despite signs it wasn't the right fit. Determined to cram my life into the box I built, I got married at 28 to someone whose career became the center of our lives and forced me and my career into the back seat.

As a coach's wife, my main priority was to support his career. I still held fast to my career dreams, but whenever I began to gain traction, we had to relocate. Multiple moves meant that I couldn't secure licensure to work as a therapist in each different state, so I eventually switched to teaching and became a professor at The University of Cincinnati. With every move, I began losing myself and focusing more on being the "coach's wife" while my dreams drifted out of focus. Once our daughter was born, my focus turned to being a great mother and I soon lost myself in that role, too.

MY TURNING POINT

Then the biggest "do-over" of all happened - divorce. I had to figure out who I was now and what I wanted the rest of my life to look like. It was clear that going back to my previous career and ideas of success no longer made sense. Life had changed me and I accepted that it was okay to reinvent myself based on my ever-changing circumstances. I now had a responsibility to think about the kind of woman I wanted to model for my daughter and to find the courage to make choices that were authentic to the best version of me. My decision to get a divorce meant giving up everything that I thought embodied success and finding a different path while finding the confidence to believe in myself again. It meant that I had to resurrect my career and decide what being a successful woman and mother would look like. I could let go of everyone else's opinions and finally decide and define what I wanted for myself.

LESSONS LEARNED

Some of the most valuable lessons I learned were:
- ➤ It's never too late to start over
- ➤ Be fearless
- ➤ Let go of the need for the validation of others

The most important thing I did was repair my relationship with the idea of being selfish. I had to embrace that the only way to be successful was to ensure that I was doing the best job of nurturing myself by understanding the true meaning of self-care. I immediately started therapy and medication to deal with the depression that had hampered my ability to

my confidence and get back into the work world. Caring for myself became my priority. I took control of my health focusing on diet, exercise, rest, and overall mental health. I became intentional about learning to listen and trust myself. Meditation and mindfulness were a huge part of my healing process.

We change when the pain of where we are becomes greater than the fear of what comes next. All of the obstacles I faced showed me that though change is scary, it doesn't have to be painful. You get to decide how you enter new experiences because anxiety and excitement are two sides of the same coin, both born from uncertainty, but your mindset determines how you approach the unknown. The best thing you can do is flow with change because it is the one certainty in life.

Surround yourself with people who empower you with accountability. Never stop making yourself the priority or let your dreams take a back seat. Know that the right partner will make room in the front seat for both of your dreams. Hold yourself accountable, always giving yourself grace and space to grow.

ACHIEVING SUCCESS

I see success through the lives changed by sharing my story and guiding others through my book and coaching program. I have used every obstacle as a springboard to the next phase of my career and accomplished things I never thought I would by starting businesses and achieving my childhood dream of writing a book. Most importantly, I learned to measure my success by the lives I touch, not by the money I make or outward accolades.

I plan to continue coaching women helping them uncover their uniqueness and leverage those strengths to achieve the life of their dreams. I will continue teaching the importance of wellness and balance, permitting women to define success for themselves.

REFLECTION AND ACTION

I challenge others to re-introduce yourself to YOU. Become intimately familiar with your gifts and begin using them more intentionally and fruitfully. Compare your life with the vision you dare to dream, and then make concrete goals to be accountable to yourself to make that vision your reality.

www.darlenetaylor.com
www.darlenetaylor.com/social-links
darlene@darlenetaylor.com

by Alina Timofeeva

FROM CLEANING TOILETS TO GLOBAL STAGES: THE EDUCATIONAL JOURNEY OF ALINA TIMOFEEVA

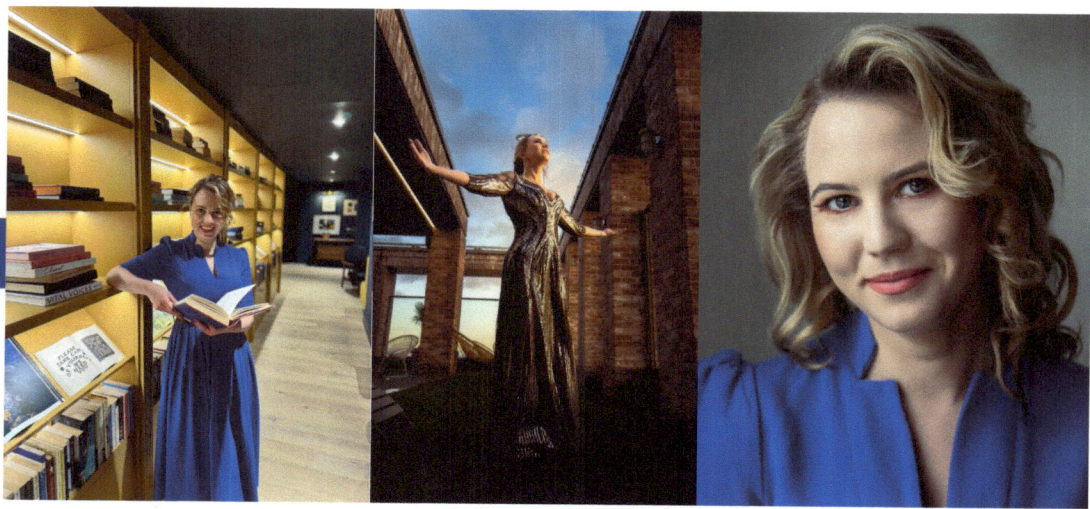

Alina Timofeeva's journey is a powerful testament to resilience and the transformative power of education. Born in a small village in post-Soviet Russia, her path from washing toilets at McDonald's in Russia to becoming a prominent figure in technology in London, UK, underscores her unwavering determination and passion for learning. This article explores Alina's educational journey, highlighting how her relentless pursuit of knowledge paved the way for her success.

EARLY BEGINNINGS AND SELF-EDUCATION

Growing up in a poor family, Alina was raised with the expectation that her future would be confined to traditional gender roles. However, she felt destined for more. Alina's thirst for knowledge became evident early on. At just eight years old, she taught herself English using old audiotapes—a skill that would become invaluable. Her academic potential was recognised when she won the prestigious Moscow State University Olympiad at 14, granting her direct admission to a specialised mathematics school. This achievement marked the beginning of a series of academic successes.

Continuing her trajectory of excellence, Alina secured another Olympiad win at 16, earning a full scholarship to Moscow State University (MSU). At MSU, she pursued both a Bachelor's and a Master's degree in Mathematics, honing her analytical and problem-solving skills in a rigorous academic environment.

EXPANDING HORIZONS AT THE LONDON SCHOOL OF ECONOMICS

Alina's academic journey extended beyond Russia. Determined to broaden her horizons, she pursued a second Master's degree in Risk and Finance at the prestigious London School of Economics (LSE). This transition came with its challenges, as she navigated the competitive UK job market, often feeling out of place among peers from more privileged backgrounds. Nevertheless, her solid academic foundation and determination saw her through these obstacles.

OVERCOMING BARRIERS

Despite her impressive educational background, Alina faced significant challenges in her early career. Navigating societal expectations and professional etiquette in the UK proved challenging. Her tenacity was tested as she applied for 500 jobs and faced 497 rejections before securing a graduate analyst position at Accenture. This experience highlighted her resilience—a hallmark of her journey.

Alina faced further challenges in her career, particularly during her first promotion attempt. With the guidance of a senior mentor, she rediscovered her confidence and self-worth, leading to a successful promotion just a year after being deemed as failing. Her perseverance paid off, as she was promoted four times in four years—an impressive feat in the male-dominated tech industry.

TENACITY SHAPING CAREER JOURNEY

Today, in her early thirties, Alina is a multi-award-winning strategic advisor in Data & Technology, serving the C-suite of major financial services organizations. She holds a board position at The Chartered Institute for IT and is a thought leader, sought-after speaker, and role model in the tech industry. Her work with leading consulting firms like Oliver Wyman, KPMG, and Accenture has earned her numerous accolades, including Digital Leader of the Year, Digital Transformation Leader, Cloud Professional of the Year, and Most Inspirational Individual of the Year.

SPEAKING ON GLOBAL STAGES

Alina has become a prominent voice on Data and Technology, speaking at high-profile events like the World Economic Forum, London Tech Week, and Money 20/20. She has also shared her insights at prestigious institutions, including the University of Oxford and the London School of Economics. Her TEDx talk, "Fail but Never Give Up," has garnered over 510,000 views, translated into 23 languages, and ranks among the top 10 most-watched TEDx talks released in December 2021. In it, she illustrates how failing an exam for a fast-food chain can lead to three university degrees, career success, and becoming a role model for women in technology.

LIFELONG LEARNING AND MENTORSHIP

Throughout her career, Alina has emphasized the importance of lifelong learning and mentorship. Her journey has taught her the significance of acquiring not just knowledge but also the ability to navigate unspoken societal codes. By seeking mentorship and continually learning, she has overcome biases and thrived in traditionally male-dominated fields.

GIVING BACK

Alina's commitment to education extends beyond her achievements. She founded Unique. Bold. You, an initiative supporting individuals from diverse backgrounds to persevere despite failures. She actively coaches others, particularly women in technology and those from underprivileged backgrounds, guiding them through their educational and professional journeys. As a TEDx speaker and LinkedIn Top Voice in Technology, she aims to inspire 50 million people globally to view failure as an opportunity for growth, whether in technology or personal endeavours.

Alina Timofeeva's educational journey serves as a powerful reminder of the transformative potential of education. From teaching herself English to excelling at two of the world's most prestigious universities, her story is one of relentless pursuit of knowledge. Alina's journey demonstrates that with determination, resilience, and a commitment to learning, one can overcome even the most daunting challenges.

FENIX TV: THE MAGIC BEHIND OUR LUXURY GIFTING SUITE FOR EMMYS WEEK

By Hanna Olivas

As the Chief Branding Officer of FENIX TV, I'm thrilled to share a glimpse of what we're preparing for this year's Emmys Week. There's a certain buzz in the air as the industry's most talented creators, storytellers, and visionaries gear up for one of the most exciting events in television: the Emmys. This year, we're elevating the celebration with our luxury gifting suite, where art, creativity, and the beauty of collaboration come together in one exclusive space.

Imagine walking the red carpet, surrounded by the energy and glamour of Hollywood's brightest stars. Our gifting suite is where the industry's top talent will gather—not just for the luxurious gifts, but to connect, celebrate, and reflect on what it takes to create television that moves, entertains, and challenges audiences. It's a rare opportunity for those who live and breathe creativity to come together and recognize the incredible artistry behind the scenes.

What I find truly inspiring about this event is that it's not just about the glitz and glamour. Yes, there will be stunning red carpet moments, but our focus is on celebrating the magic behind the camera—the untold stories of the creative process. There's something profoundly fascinating about understanding what it takes to bring a show or film to life. Most people see the finished product, but the real magic happens in the countless hours of writing, designing, editing, and collaborating to create something exceptional.

At FENIX TV, we want to shine a spotlight on the unsung heroes—the screenwriters who pour their hearts into scripts, the directors who bring stories to life, the set designers who transform ideas into immersive worlds, and the sound engineers who make every note resonate. The Emmy nominees we honor this year represent the best of this craft. They're not just talented individuals; they're visionaries who have pushed the boundaries of what television can be. Their work challenges conventions, tells bold stories, and leaves an indelible mark on the industry.

One of the things I'm most excited about is offering a behind-the-scenes look at what really goes into making a show or film. We're opening a window into the creative process, revealing the dedication, collaboration, and artistry that many people never get to see. The Television Academy and the Emmys are more than just a night of awards—they're a celebration of the countless hours of work, the late nights, the breakthroughs, and the passion that drive this industry.

Our luxury gifting suite is designed to be a place where art, luxury, and inspiration converge. We've curated a collection of premium gifts from brands that align with our vision of creativity and excellence. But more than that, we want this space to be one where those who've dedicated their lives to storytelling can take a moment to reflect, recharge, and connect with like-minded creators.

As I look forward to this event, I can't help but feel a deep sense of excitement and pride. The Emmy's Week gifting suite is more than just an event; it's a celebration of the craft that I hold close to my heart. It's about honoring the brilliance that happens behind the scenes, the unsung work that leads to those shining moments on stage.

This year's Emmys aren't just a recognition of talent; they're a tribute to the power of storytelling, the creativity that drives our industry, and the extraordinary individuals who make it all possible. We can't wait to celebrate with you and share this incredible experience. After all, it's moments like these that remind us why we fell in love with television and film in the first place—because of the stories that move us, the art that inspires us, and the people who make it all come alive.

SEPTEMBER 13, 2024

SHE RISES STUDIOS   FENIX TV

SAVANNAH KENNICK
ACTRESS

CHRIS BEAL
CO-PRODUCER, EMMY NOMINATED
SERIES, PEACOCK'S, "BEL AIR"

ROCKET MINJIZZLE
CELEBRITY MAKEUP ARTIST/
INFLUENCER & RED CARPET
CORRESPONDENT

DANA HICKS-HUNGERFORD
ACTRESS AND DESIGNER

KIKI SHEPARD
ACTRESS, BOUNCE TV'S,
"MIND YOUR BUSINESS"/
TV PERSONALITY/PHILANTHROPIST

ARELI MADRIGAL
SOCAL LATINA LIFESTYLE/BEAUTY
CONTENT CREATOR/INFLUENCER

GABRIELLE REECE
VOLLEYBALL PLAYER, SPORTS
ANNOUNCER, FASHION MODEL,
ACTRESS AND PRODUCER

FENIX TV EMMYS WEEK

PREMIER GIFTING
Suite

4 STEPS TO HEAL EMOTIONAL PAIN WITH SELF-LOVE

FEEL, BREATHE, EXPRESS, RECEIVE

By Brett Cotter

The first step is walk toward everything you've been running from. To sit with your emotions like you're sitting with an old friend and have compassion for your feelings like you're consoling a young child.

"As a clinician, it was impressive feeling my own stress lift out of my body." Gerri DeBenedetto, LCSW, NY

The easiest way I found to feel painful emotions is to touch the tension in your body with your hand whenever you are upset. Emotional tension usually resides in the chest, stomach, solar-plexus, or throat. Touch creates a connection that helps the cells stuck in the painful past return to the present moment.

Tightness in your heart reflects anger or sadness around being disconnected from love. Tension in your stomach results from pushing your emotions down. Tightness in your solar-plexus is caused by having your power taken away or giving it away. And tension in your throat comes from not speaking your truth.

"I was depressed and suicidal. In 45 minutes that all changed. I learned how to cope with PTSD and be at peace within myself. I owe my life to him." Rick Williamson, Army Veteran, Peer Support Specialist, MT

The second step is breathe deep and slow into the center of the tightness by focusing your attention on the tension as you breathe. You are now delivering life-force energy into the center of the tightness and the cake begins to bake as the ball of emotional pain unwinds and expands.

The third step is express all your feelings that are wrapped up in this pain. If you find yourself repeating statements you're caught in a loop. Switch it up. Initially expressing what the pain feels like, where it is in your body, and what triggered it. Then going deeper expressing where it might be stemming from by verbalizing some details about the first time ever in your life, you can remember having this feeling. You can reflect on the household you grew up in and the family members that were with you. Let those deeper feelings arise and express in a stream of consciousness without sensor or judgement. I call this emptying the tank. Real emotional healing is not about the trigger, it's about the trauma.

"I was wrapped in the love and presence of my deceased son, grandma and grandpa. It was so peaceful. He has a God-given gift." Sandra Henderson, Ret. Hospice Ast.

Once you've expressed all the built up emotions then move to the fourth step, receive. Finally the fun part. It's fun because it's full of miracles. As you touch the tension, breathe deep and slow, insert your favorite word to refer to a higher power and say, "____ shine your light right through the center of my [insert the location of your tension], unlock and release all this [insert the type of emotion you feel], right now. I reclaim my true identity, just as the creator created me. I am free for all eternity." Repeating this statement slowly for 10-15 minutes while touching the tension will release the emotional pain from your body. If you're wondering, "Why is step 4 named Receive?" "What did I receive?" The answer is your true self.

I just gave you the formula. If you want me to do it for ya, come to our next retreat to experience life-changing, lasting relief. You suffered long enough, just meet me halfway. Show up, I will guide you, and spirit will melt your pain away. www.StressIsGone.com

REACH ME

STRESS IS GONE
with Brett Cotter

Breaking Barriers: Transforming Adversity into Leadership as an Immigrant Woman

by Tamanna Ramesh

A decade ago, a determined young woman from a small town in India arrived in the United States, fueled by dreams of a better future. Despite the promise of new opportunities, her journey was fraught with challenges—cultural adjustments, language barriers, workplace toxicity, and the complexities of the U.S. immigration system. Yet, her unwavering commitment to personal and professional growth powered her through these obstacles.

From the outset, integrating into the American workplace proved difficult due to cultural differences and the complex immigration system. The Green Card process was particularly daunting, with the EB2 category's wait time exceeding 130 years—a formidable barrier. Professionally, she faced pay equity issues and the constant need to prove herself, especially as a woman in STEM. These obstacles were compounded by harassment, discrimination, and the everyday stress of navigating a new country. Nevertheless, she transformed these adversities into opportunities for growth.

Her journey was marked by an impressive achievement: securing $135,000 in scholarships and assistantships, which funded her STEM graduate degree and part-time MBA program in the U.S. This financial support was crucial, allowing her to focus on her education without incurring significant debt. Over the years, she honed her networking strategies and perfected her negotiation tactics, landing dream jobs at Fortune 500 companies and making five unconventional career pivots. Each move was a calculated step towards building her personal brand and significantly increasing her compensation.

A defining moment in her life came when she secured her Green Card at the age of 29, breaking through the historic wait time barrier by qualifying under the EB1 category—one of the most challenging categories for Indian nationals. This achievement was not just a personal victory but a profound symbol of new beginnings. Free from immigration uncertainty, she could finally pursue her aspirations fully.

With renewed determination, she committed to continuous personal and professional development, advancing from a researcher to a director at a Fortune 100 company. This remarkable progression was driven by hard work, perseverance, and the invaluable support of mentors and sponsors who nurtured her potential. She also took on leadership roles in professional organizations, notably with the Institute of Food Technologists, where she served as Chair of the Product Development Division and the Women's Resource Group. These roles amplified her influence and established her as a thought leader in the food and beverage industry.

Throughout her journey, she faced numerous unseen challenges: overperforming while underpaid, dealing with bad managers, experiencing burnout and imposter syndrome, and confronting biases and systemic barriers. While the highs on her LinkedIn profile are visible, the lows—marked by harassment, bullying, and the grueling immigration process—were equally significant. Despite these struggles, she chose to fight, paving her own path with resilience and determination.

Her experiences taught her that success is not solely defined by titles or financial gain but by the freedom and empowerment to pursue one's own path. Perseverance, adaptability, and continuous learning were essential to overcoming adversity and achieving success.

To those navigating similar challenges, she advises remaining resilient and proactive. Seek out mentors and sponsors for guidance and support, and invest in continuous learning to enhance your skills and adaptability. Challenges often present opportunities for significant personal growth and success.

Today, she stands as a leader at a Fortune 100 company and the founder of Spark Career Services, dedicated to supporting underrepresented individuals in their career journeys. Through Spark Career Services, she helps others overcome barriers, achieve career advancement, and drive equity in the workplace. Her goal is to empower one million individuals to break through barriers and achieve career fulfillment, with a commitment to fostering workplace wellness and championing purpose-driven careers.

Call to Action for All the Amazing Women Out There:

- **ASK** for those high-visibility projects, raises, and promotions that you deserve.
- **BALANCE** by prioritizing your well-being to avoid burnout and undue stress.
- **CHALLENGE** biases and systemic barriers that stand in your way.

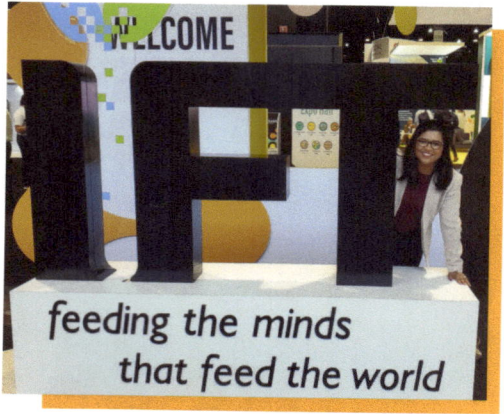

feeding the minds that feed the world

Contact:
www.sparkcareerservices.com
www.linkedin.com/company/spark-career-services
www.linkedin.com/in/tamannaramesh
www.instagram.com/spark_your_career

sparkcareerservicesllc@gmail.com

by Angelica Kapsis

PIONEERING VETERAN TRANSFORMING U.S. ELECTIONS

Angelica Kapsis, President of VotRite

Angelica Kapsis is the President and Co-Founder of VotRite, a South Florida company dedicated to re-shaping how elections are conducted in the United States. With Angelica at the helm, VotRite is determined to make the future of local, state, and national elections more accessible, more secure, and more transparent for all. VotRite is also committed to maintaining an environment free from bullying and harassment. Angelica ensures her team is treated with dignity while being held to above higher than average standards for their performance.

Angelica is a dedicated professional with a diverse background in forensic science, psychology, and human services. She holds a Masters in Science in Forensic Science from National University as well as a Bachelor of Science in Psychology from Stony Brook University, showcasing her strong commitment to education and continuous learning.

In addition to her incredible academic career, Angelica is an accomplished Navy Veteran. She has built her life and career on fighting for those in need. As the President and Co-Founder of VotRite, Angelica has been instrumental in developing strategies to enhance voting software accessibility, particularly focusing on ADA (Americans with Disabilities Act) compliance and preferences for individuals with disabilities.

Angelica is also the Founder at Scorpion Fitness Centers, a position that reflects her passion for promoting health and wellness. She has crafted unique fitness plans for members and leads classes, including those catered to individuals with disabilities, in order to guarantee success for clients.

Beyond her professional endeavors, Angelica's dedication to community service is evident through her involvement in various volunteer activities. Angelica has worked as a firefighter, a mentor, and has advocated for at-risk populations. She is also a NASM Certified Personal Trainer and holds CPR & First Aid Certification. Angelica's multifaceted skill set, coupled with her unwavering dedication to social causes, positions her as a versatile and compassionate professional dedicated to making a truly positive impact in her community and beyond.

Angelica is a passionate advocate for technological innovation and creativity. Her company, VotRite, stands at the forefront of electoral innovation, offering cutting-edge voting solutions designed to revolutionize the democratic process. Committed to inclusivity and integrity, VotRite ensures that every voter, regardless of ability or background, can participate in hack-proof elections with confidence. With a steadfast dedication to neutrality and transparency, VotRite's unbiased approach guarantees that election results are trustworthy and immune to contestation. By prioritizing ADA compliance, customizable features, and a commitment to impartiality, VotRite is leading the charge towards fair and equitable elections, where every voice is heard and every vote counts.

To work beside her in achieving her mission, Angelica has selected only those that share her passionate dream and have the knowledge to follow through. Jim Kapsis, VotRite's CEO, has extensive management and technology capabilities and has been the leader of various voting companies in the last 30 years. He has created two patents for voting integration and copyright software. Christopher H. Baum, the company's Chief Compliance Officer, has spent more than 30 years delivering high-quality IT analysis and services on the use of technology in government and in the election industry in particular. Baum currently manages certification processes and ensures election integrity.

As of 2024, VotRite has been officially nominated for this year's Technology Innovator Awards hosted by Innovation in Business, as well as nominated for the 2024 Education and Training Awards hosted by Corporate Vision. It is because of Angelica's unwavering dedication and determination that her company has achieved success, and she has persevered in spite of pushback from other Electronic Voting Machine organizations. Angelica has offered her knowledge and expertise to a variety of media outlets, including the podcast Everyday's Saturday - USMC Veteran and Authority Magazine. She will also be featured in upcoming episodes of the HomeFront Sitrep Podcast as well as the Implementors Podcast.

by Kay Harper

FROM FARM ROOTS TO COUNTRY MUSIC'S RISING STAR

I grew up in a small farming town in southern Michigan, a place where hard work was the way of life. My grandfather was a third-generation dairy farmer, and my parents ran a vegetable farm, teaching me the value of perseverance and dedication from a young age. My early life was filled with the sounds of country music legends like Patsy Cline and Loretta Lynn, which sparked my passion for music. I sang in school choirs, taught myself guitar through online tutorials, and dreamed of a future where my voice could be heard by the world.

However, life wasn't always kind. My childhood was marked by the absence of my biological father and the presence of an abusive and manipulative step-dad. Feeling the sting of abandonment and dealing with the traumas of a turbulent homelife left deep scars. The emotional turmoil led to significant self-esteem and anger issues that plagued me for years.

The challenges continued to mount during my senior year of high school when I lost a friend to suicide. This was a devastating blow, especially since I was also struggling with my own mental health and had been considering suicide as well. Shortly after, I found myself pregnant at 18, trapped in a toxic relationship and repeating the same cycles from my childhood. By 25, I was divorced and trying to navigate life as a single mother, all while dealing with the fallout of my unresolved traumas and a near diagnosis of borderline personality disorder.

Also, the compilation of no's from singing contests and the reality TV industry (The Voice, AGT, and American Idol) continued to wear on me as well. Although I had been close multiple times even gaining private interviews with producers, I ultimately always received a no. I was in this headspace where I thought the only way to make it was to be noticed by these people and each no was a letdown.

The turning point in my journey came when I hit the age of 30. Realizing that life was passing me by, I knew I had to take control of my destiny. It was a moment of self-reckoning where I decided that enough was enough. I could no longer wait for a miracle or validation from the outside world.

I began to actively pursue my passion for music, starting with local gigs and open mic nights. This was a huge step for someone who had always struggled with anxiety and body image issues. I also sought therapy during my divorce and after to address my mental health challenges, which helped me develop coping mechanisms and a healthier mindset. Reconnecting with my biological father & biological family provided some closure and helped me understand and forgive the past.

In addition to my musical pursuits, I leveraged my professional skills in marketing and PR to build my brand. I taught myself how to handle everything from photoshoots to social media management, ensuring that I had complete control over my career. The culmination of these efforts was recording my debut single, "Freight Train," in Nashville with the help of some incredibly talented musicians.

One of the most important lessons I learned is the power of resilience. Despite the setbacks and challenges, each "no" I received from reality TV shows like American Idol and The Voice only fueled my determination. I also learned the importance of self-belief and taking proactive steps toward my goals. Waiting for someone else to recognize your worth is a path to nowhere; you have to be your own biggest advocate.

For those facing similar challenges, my advice is to never give up on your dreams. Take actionable steps, no matter how small, toward your goals. Seek out support systems, whether it's therapy, friends, or family, and don't be afraid to ask for help. Remember that setbacks are just setups

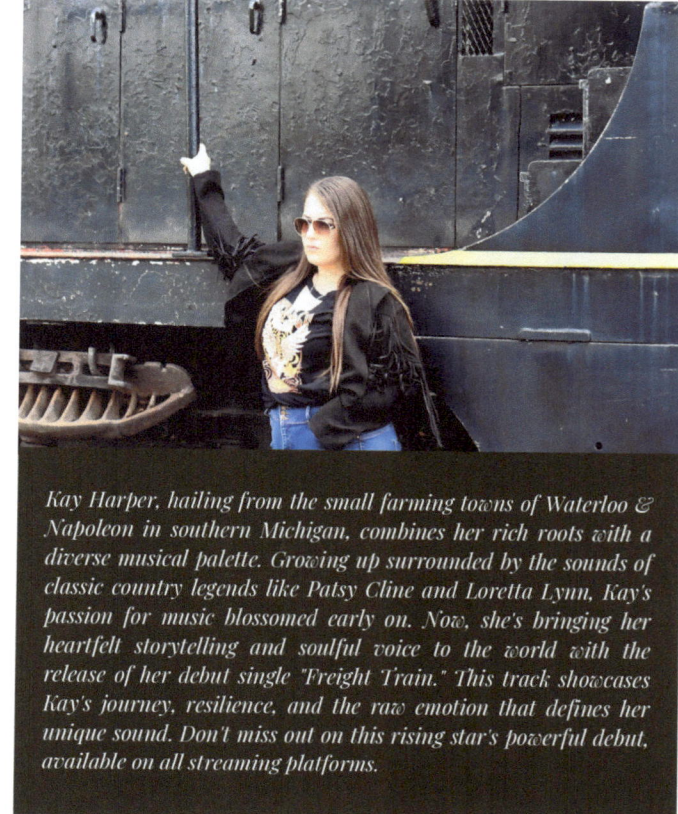

Kay Harper, hailing from the small farming towns of Waterloo & Napoleon in southern Michigan, combines her rich roots with a diverse musical palette. Growing up surrounded by the sounds of classic country legends like Patsy Cline and Loretta Lynn, Kay's passion for music blossomed early on. Now, she's bringing her heartfelt storytelling and soulful voice to the world with the release of her debut single "Freight Train." This track showcases Kay's journey, resilience, and the raw emotion that defines her unique sound. Don't miss out on this rising star's powerful debut, available on all streaming platforms.

for comebacks. Use your experiences, no matter how painful, as fuel to propel you forward.

Today, I am proud to say that I am thriving both personally and professionally. "Freight Train" has been well-received, and I continue to perform and connect with audiences who find solace and inspiration in my music. Overcoming adversity has not only contributed to my success but also shaped me into a stronger, more compassionate individual.

Looking ahead, I aim to continue making music that resonates with people and tells authentic stories of struggle and triumph. I want to use my platform to advocate for mental health awareness and support others who are dealing with similar challenges. My goal is to inspire others to believe in themselves and pursue their dreams, no matter the obstacles.

I encourage you, the reader, to reflect on your own challenges and consider how you can turn them into opportunities for growth. Take that first step toward overcoming your obstacles and remember that you are not alone. By sharing our stories and supporting one another, we can create a world where resilience and perseverance lead to incredible achievements.

www.kayharperofficial.com
www.facebook.com/kayharperofficial
www.instagram.com/kayharperofficial
www.tiktok.com/kayharperofficial
www.distrokid.com/hyperfollow/kayharper/freight-train

The SHE RISES STUDIOS PODCAST

The She Rises Studios podcast is dedicated to empowering women like you to reach their full potential and live their best lives. With inspiring stories, insightful interviews, and practical advice from experts in different industries, our podcast is your go-to source for information, inspiration, and motivation. Join us as we explore topics like:

- Overcoming self-doubt and limiting beliefs
- Building and running a successful business
- Building confidence and Self-esteem
- Navigating career transitions
- Starting and growing a business
- Balancing work and family life
- Improving physical and mental health
- Finding meaning and purpose in life
- So many more

Our guests include successful entrepreneurs, inspiring thought leaders, and everyday women who have overcome challenges and achieved their dreams. Each episode is packed with actionable tips and strategies to help you take your life to the next level.